THE NATURE KIDS GUIDE TO

KANGAROOS

DAVID ANDERSON

LP Media Inc. Publishing
Text copyright © 2026 by LP Media Inc.
All rights reserved.

For information address LP Media Inc. Publishing,
30012 Variolite St NW, Princeton MN 55371
www.lpmedia.org

Publication Data

Kangaroos
The Nature Kid's Guide to Kangaroos — First edition.

Summary: "Learn all about Kangaroos, the Nature Kid Way"
— Provided by publisher.

ISBN: 979-8-89818-125-3

[1. Kangaroos – Non-Fiction] I. Title.

Title: The Nature Kid's Guide to Kangaroos

CONTENTS

OUTBACK HOME

Red kangaroos can cover 25 feet in a single hop. That is longer than a school bus!

Thump! A kangaroo lands in dry grass. Its big ears turn to listen.

Kangaroos live in many different environments. Some hop through hot, dry deserts. The ground is dusty and red. Trees are far apart. These kangaroos find shade when the sun is too hot.

Other kangaroos live in cool forests. Tall trees give them shelter. Soft grass grows on the ground. They munch on green leaves.

Some kangaroos like open grasslands. The land is flat and wide. Fresh water sits in small ponds nearby. Kangaroos need water to drink and plants to eat. Each type of kangaroo picks the **habitat** that feels just right.

AUSSIE ANIMALS

Rustle! A grey kangaroo hops through tall bushes. Her joey peeks out.

Kangaroos live only in Australia and Tasmania

Red kangaroos live in the dry middle of Australia. Grey kangaroos live near the coasts.

Eastern grey kangaroos live on the east side. Western grey kangaroos live on the west side.

Tasmania only has Forester kangaroos, which are similar to the Eastern Grey kangaroos in Australia. Red Kangaroos do not live there.

Wallabies look like miniature kangaroos but are actually a completely different species!

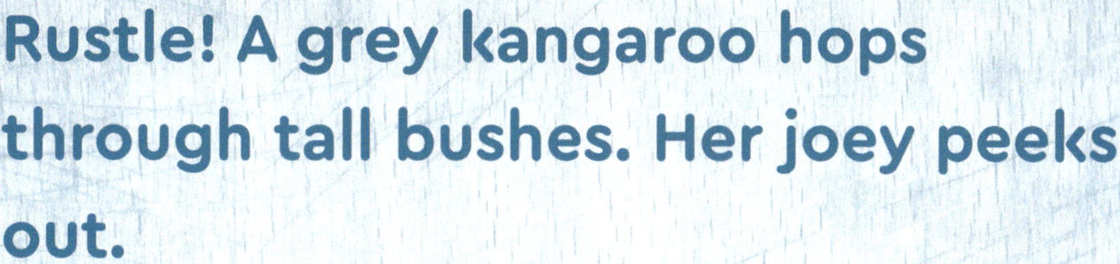

SUPER SIZED

Whoosh! A red kangaroo hops through the outback.

Red kangaroos are the biggest kangaroos in the world. Males can stand over six feet tall. That is taller than most adults! They can weigh up to 200 pounds.

Female red kangaroos are much smaller. They weigh about half as much as males.

Grey kangaroos are a bit smaller than red kangaroos. But they are still big animals. A male grey kangaroo can weigh over 140 pounds.

Female red kangaroos actually have have blue-gray fur. Their nickname is "Blue Flyers"!

BUILT TO BOUNCE

Boing! A kangaroo springs high into the air. It lands softly and hops again.

Kangaroos have bodies made for hopping. Their back legs are long and very strong. Their big feet help them push off the ground.

A kangaroo's tail is thick and muscular. It helps them balance when they hop. The tail also holds them up when they stand still.

Kangaroos have short front legs. These small arms help them grab food. They also use them to groom their fur. Their whole body works together to help them move fast.

EARS UP

Snap! A grey kangaroo's ears twist backward. It heard something move.

Kangaroos have excellent hearing. Their big ears can turn in different directions. Each ear moves on its own. This helps them hear sounds from all around.

Kangaroos also have great eyesight. Their eyes sit on the sides of their head. This lets them see almost all the way around.

These senses help kangaroos stay safe.

Because their eyes are spread far apart, Kangaroos have a blind spot right in front of their nose!

KICK BACK

14

Wham! A kangaroo kicks hard with both feet. Watch out for those claws!

Kangaroos can defend themselves with powerful kicks. They lean back on their strong tails. Then they strike with both back feet at once.

Their sharp claws make kicks even more dangerous. Each back foot has a long, pointed claw.

Kangaroos also use their front paws to scratch and grab attackers. Many animals avoid fighting kangaroos.

Kangaroos cannot walk backward! Their long tail and big back feet stop them.

GRASS
GRAZERS

Crunch! A kangaroo bites off some grass. Then it chews slowly.

Kangaroos eat mostly grass. They are **grazers**, like cows and sheep. They spend many hours each day eating.

Kangaroos have special teeth for eating plants. These flat back teeth grind up tough grass. When the teeth wear down, new ones grow in.

Kangaroos get most of their water from plants. This helps them live in dry places. Red kangaroos only need to drink water about twice a week!

Kangaroos have a stomach with four sections just like cows!

SPEAKING KANGAROO

A mother kangaroo can hear her joey's call even in a large group of other kangaroos.

Thump! A kangaroo pounds the ground with its foot.

Kangaroos make many sounds. They use their bodies to send messages too.

Mothers and joeys click and cluck. This helps them find each other.

Male kangaroos make a cough sound. This tells other males to stay away. Females make soft clicks. They call their babies this way.

Kangaroos use their bodies to talk too. They stomp their big back feet. The loud thump warns others. It means danger is near. The sound goes far across the land.

WATCH OUT

Growl! A dingo spots a kangaroo. The kangaroo hears it and stands alert.

Kangaroos face danger from predators. Dingoes are wild dogs. They hunt kangaroos in Australia. They often chase young or weak ones.

Wedge-tailed eagles fly above. These big birds can attack joeys. Pythons are a danger too. They sometimes catch small kangaroos.

But humans are their biggest threat. Cars hit many kangaroos at night. Kangaroos freeze when they see bright lights.

Dingoes hunt in packs of up to twelve dogs to catch large kangaroos.

HOP AWAY

Swoosh! A kangaroo bounds away fast. Dust flies behind it.

Kangaroos hop away from danger. Their strong back legs help them leap far. They can turn fast while they hop.

Kangaroos hop towards water when chased. They are good swimmers. A dingo cannot catch a kangaroo in the water.

Living in groups keeps kangaroos safe. Many eyes watch for danger. One kangaroo thumps its foot. This warns the others.

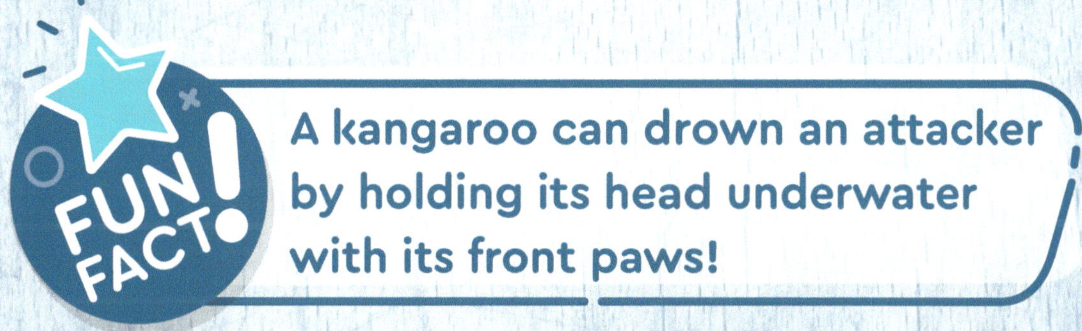

A kangaroo can drown an attacker by holding its head underwater with its front paws!

BOING BOING

Pounce! A kangaroo leaps across a field. Its tail swings for balance.

Kangaroos are some of the best jumpers in the world. They are the largest animals that hop to get around. They use their big back legs to jump. Their long tail helps them balance.

Kangaroos can hop very fast. They reach speeds of 35 miles per hour. They cover up to 25 feet in one leap.

Hopping saves energy. Their tendons work like springs.

Kangaroos use their tail like a fifth leg. They push off the ground with it to help walk.

COOL CREW

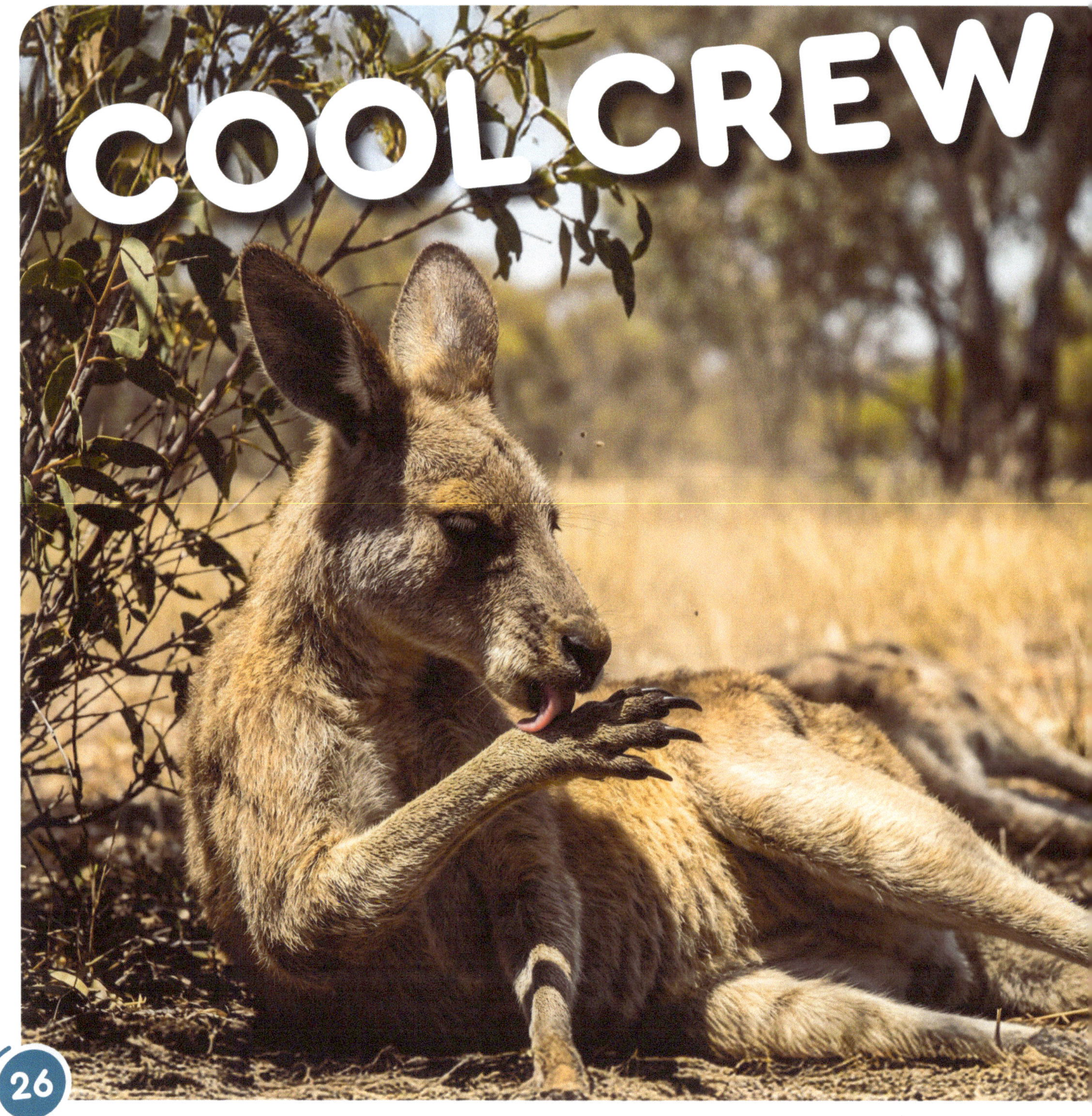

Lick! A kangaroo rests in the shade. It slowly licks its arms to cool off.

Kangaroos stay cool in hot weather. They rest during the day when the sun is strong. They find shade under trees or bushes.

Kangaroos lick their arms to cool down. Their arms have special blood vessels near the skin. The wet saliva helps lower body heat.

Kangaroos also dig shallow holes in cool soil. They lie in they cool dirt and nap.

Kangaroos pant like dogs when they get very hot. They also sweat a little while hopping.

MOB RULES

Click! A kangaroo calls to its group. Others hop closer.

Kangaroos live in groups called **mobs**. A mob usually has between ten and one hundred kangaroos.

Mobs have a leader. The biggest male is usually in charge. He is called the **dominant** male.

Females and their joeys stay close together in the mob. Young males often live in small groups or alone.

Kangaroos groom each other in their mobs. They use their paws to clean each other's fur.

BOXING BATTLES

Grunt! Two male kangaroos stand face to face. They push each other.

Male kangaroos sometimes fight. They push and wrestle with their arms. This is called boxing.

Males box to show strength. The strongest male leads the mob. He uses his size to win.

Kangaroos lean back on their tails during fights. This lets them kick with their strong back legs. Fights can be short or long, but one male always hops away.

Male kangaroos grow arm muscles as they age. Older males have very strong front legs.

TINY JOEYS

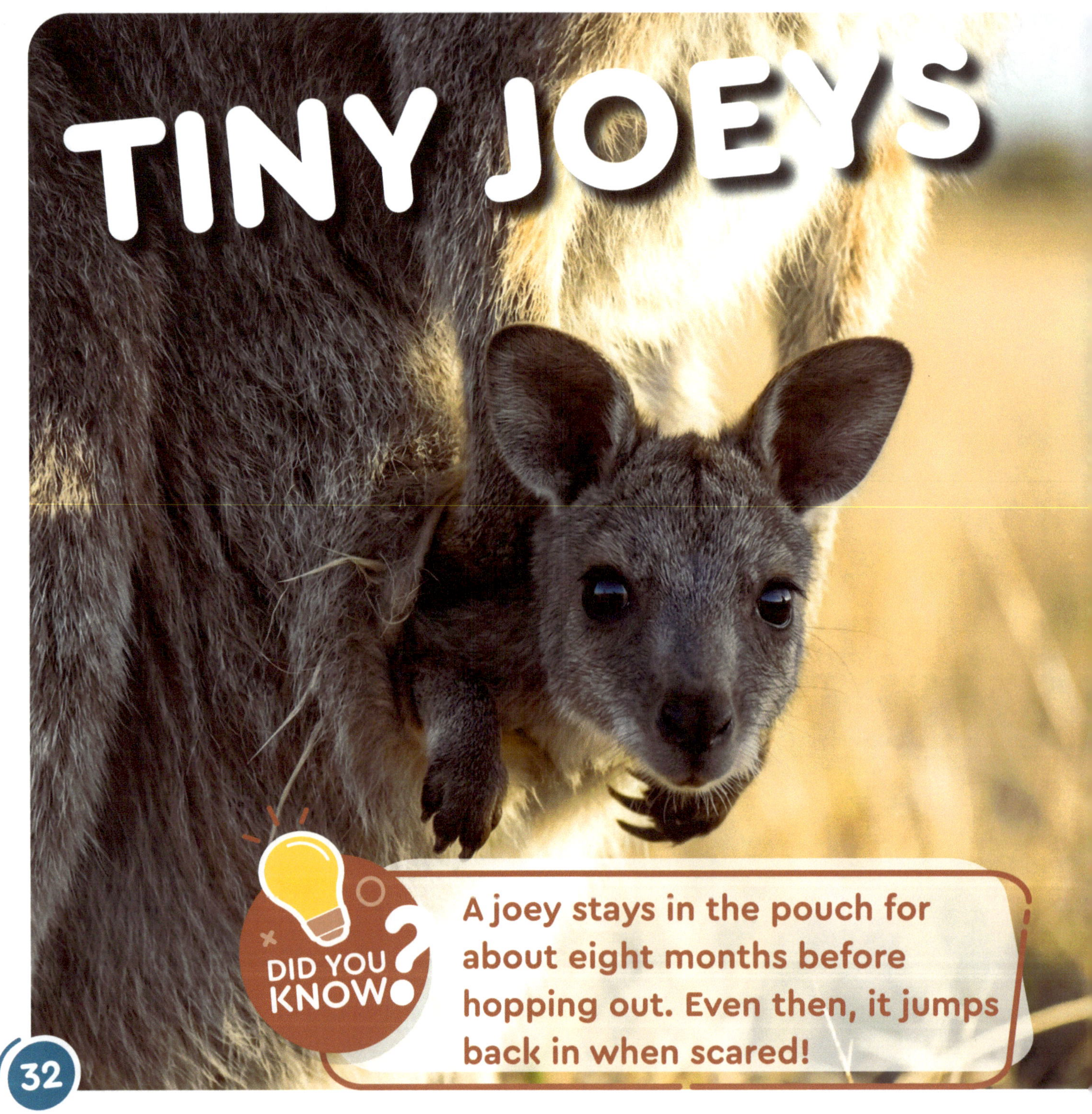

DID YOU KNOW?
A joey stays in the pouch for about eight months before hopping out. Even then, it jumps back in when scared!

Squeak! A tiny joey peeks out of the pouch. It has been in there a long time!

A newborn joey is very tiny. It is about the size of a jellybean. At this stage, it has no fur and cannot see.

The joey crawls into its mother's pouch right after birth. This trip takes about three minutes. To make the climb, the joey uses its small front legs.

Inside the pouch, the joey drinks milk. It stays attached to a nipple for many weeks. The joey grows fur and opens its eyes after about five months.

POUCH POWER

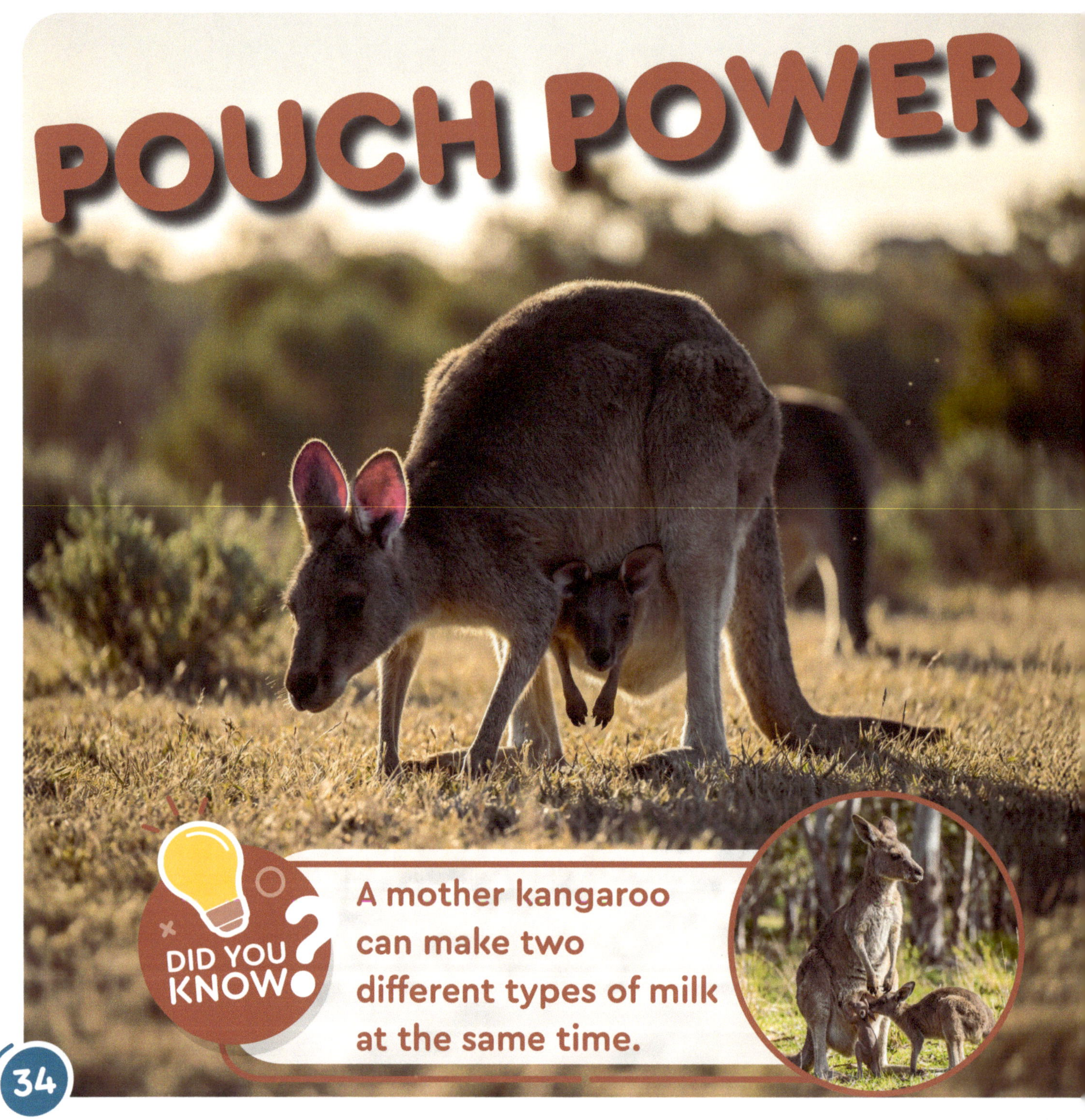

DID YOU KNOW?
A mother kangaroo can make two different types of milk at the same time.

Snort! A mother kangaroo bends down. Her joey pops out to play.

The pouch is a warm and safe place to grow. It keeps the joey protected. The pouch stretches as the joey gets bigger inside.

A joey stays in this cozy space for about six months. Then it starts to peek out and explore.

Young joeys hop out to play and learn. They nibble on grass and practice hopping. They watch their mother and copy what she does. When they get scared or tired, they jump back in the pouch.

A joey leaves the pouch for good between eight and eleven months old.

BOUNCING
BACK

Thump! A kangaroo lands hard on the dusty ground.

When new settlers came to Australia, the land changed a lot. People cut down forests to make farms. They built fences and roads. Many animals struggled to survive.

But kangaroos did well. The new grasslands were perfect for grazing. Farmers added water holes that kangaroos could drink from. There were also fewer dingoes to hunt them.

Today there are more kangaroos than ever before. Over 50 million live in Australia!

Kangaroos found ways to live alongside people. They are true survivors.

FINDING ROOS

Hop! A kangaroo gets up from a nap. He lives at the zoo!

You do not have to go to Australia to see kangaroos! Many zoos in the United States have them. Some zoos let you walk right into the kangaroo area. You can get very close and even feed them.

Wildlife parks are another great place to visit. Some have large open spaces where kangaroos hop around. You can watch them rest, eat, and play with their joeys.

Kangaroos are calm animals, but move slowly and speak softly. This helps them stay relaxed. You might even see a joey peeking out of its mother's pouch!

GLOSSARY

dominant
The one who is the leader or in charge of a group.

grazers
Animals that eat grass and other plants growing on the ground.

mob
A group of kangaroos, usually between 10–100

outback
A big, dry, dusty area in Australia where not many people live.

habitat
The type of place where an animal lives.